Bears

Bears

DANIEL WOOD

whitecap

Edited by Elizabeth McLean
Reviewed by Séan Sharpe, Carnivore Biologist
Research by Beverley Sinclair
Cover design by Steve Penner
Interior design and typesetting by Margaret Ng
Cover photograph by Thomas Kitchin/First Light

Printed and bound in Canada.

Library and Archives Canada Cataloguing in Publication
Wood, Daniel
      Bears / Daniel Wood.
Includes bibliographical references and index.

ISBN 1-55285-663-1

      1. Bears--North America. I. Title.
QL737.C27W66 2005   599.78'097   C2004-906728-1

Up there on Huckleberry Mountain, I couldn't sleep....As the sky broke light over the peaks of Glacier, I found myself deeply moved by the view from our elevation—off west the lights of Montana, Hungry Horse, and Columbia Falls, and farmsteads along the northern edge of Flathead Lake, and back in the direction of sunrise the soft and misted valleys of the parklands, not an electric light showing: little enough to preserve for the wanderings of a great and sacred animal who can teach us, if nothing else, by his power and his dilemma, a little common humility.

—William Kittredge
"Grizzly"

PREVIOUS PAGES: *In the alpine and tundra regions of Alaska, the* sik sik—*the Inuit name for the ground squirrel—is the grizzly's favorite meal. These gopherlike animals live in subterranean burrows, but when caught above ground, as here, they provide both a tasty snack and a lesson for a young cub. Unlike the wolf, the bear seldom pursues its prey for more than 100 metres (330 feet) since most small, fleeing animals can quickly out-maneuver the lumbering bear.*

C O N T E N T S

INTRODUCTION

THE BEAR: OUT OF THE WILDERNESS AND INTO THE HUMAN PSYCHE

Whenever the bear lumbers across the path of North American travelers and into human imagination, it arrives with the force of an omen. It is seldom ignored. Its presence is seen by some as an unexpected and delightful epiphany. And by others as a threat and reason for panic. The bear's reputation for unprovoked charges and the killing of humans is—on occasion—deserved. But this behavior is extremely rare. When viewed instead from a safe vantagepoint, the bear is a wonder of roundness and fluidity. Its shambling flat-footed gait, its amiable curiosity, and its long connection to some of the most enduring characters of childhood fiction foster, in fact, an assumption that the wild bear is nothing more than an oversized Winnie-the-Pooh or a Paddington with claws. This is not true. Between the hugely exaggerated lore of the bear as a wilderness terrorist and the bear of myth and fables lives the real bear: a loner for much of its life, a meditative creature, a wanderer far smarter than previously credited,

PREVIOUS PAGE, LEFT: *The bear is one of the most adaptive of all animals. Its habits and temperament vary greatly from one creature to the next, as if its solitary life has fostered a wide variety of "personalities" within the species.*

PREVIOUS PAGE, RIGHT: *These bear footprints and the imprint of Vibram-soled hiking boots spell out a warning to back-packers in northwestern North America. Capable of quick acceleration to the speed of the fastest racehorse, a grizzly cannot be outrun. Avoidance of dangerous situations, such as storing food in a tent or coming near to a mother with cubs, is the best way to mini-mize trouble.*

an animal whose winter hibernation is still surrounded with mystery, a dutiful mother, a survivor of centuries of human predation, and the largest terrestrial carnivore on Earth.

Of the eight species of bear worldwide, three range across wide expanses of North America: from the black bear's southernmost retreat in Florida's cypress swamps to the brown bear's salmon-rich streams of coastal British Columbia to the far-wandering polar bear of the high arctic ice. Because of their unpredictable nature and size—brown bears and polar bears have weighed in at 650-plus kilograms (1430 pounds)—they have held a fascination for humans since earliest times. Neolithic humans depicted them in European caves 30 000 years ago and the Asiatic explorers of North America, crossing the Bering Strait during the Ice Age, 12 500 years ago, had to contend with monstrous—and now extinct—bears the size of small cars. The bear's history, of course, goes back much further.

As the lineage of the bear developed during the last 30 million years, some became miniature—such as the prehistoric, raccoon-sized dawn bear. Others became gargantuan like the recently extinct, 1000-kilogram (2200-pound) North American short-faced bear,

LEFT: *The black bear rules the forests of North America, just as the brown bear rules the higher alpine regions, the tundra, and the coastal estuaries of the northwest. Here an Alaskan black bear explores a fallen rainforest log in its perpetual search for food.*

the largest mammalian carnivore to have walked the Earth. The Ursidae, as the bear family is scientifically known, spread over much of the planet thanks to its evolutionary divergence from the rest of the toothy, carnivore clan. While most other meat-eaters have restricted their diet to fresh prey, most species of bear gradually adapted to an omnivorous diet, eating grasses, nuts, and berries during the lush summer and fall months and eating fish, insects, and carrion when available. This dietary shift accompanied a change in the bear's teeth over the millenia as cusps for grinding vegetation came to replace sharper molars. This shift included, as well, an increased ability of the bear to consume daily—especially in the fall—huge amounts of plant material. It also explains the population explosion that began five million years ago among bear species as they fanned out with their newly acquired ability to forage in territorial niches previously off-limits. The spectacled bear of South America, the sun bear of Southeast Asia, the panda of mountainous China, the sloth bear of the Asian subcontinent, and the Himalayan black bear scattered across the Earth.

The tree-loving black bear *(Ursus americanus)* conquered most of the forested North American continent, later retreating in the face of human agriculture to Canada and 32 American states, where it is found today. Small pockets of the black bear also survive in the bayous of the southeastern United States. But the black bear has been a victim of a widespread slaughter that began well before Davy Crockett, a legendary early nineteenth-century bear-hunter, "kill'd him" not one, but hundreds in a misguided effort to rid the East of the creature. The brown bear *(Ursus arctos)* came to occupy much of

Europe, northern Asia, and—when the Ice Age freezing of the Bering Strait permitted it 30 000 years ago—the western half of North America, as far south as central Mexico. Since this expansion, however, the brown bear has in the last hundred years been driven out of Mexico and most of the 48 contiguous American states, occupying today just one percent of its former range there. It now numbers fewer than 1000 south of the 49th parallel, a population isolated along the U.S.-Canada border and in Yellowstone National Park. The polar bear *(Ursus maritimus)*, the largest of all living bears, evolved in the last 200 000 years when a group of brown bears apparently became separate from the parent stock. Adapting through color, body shape, and gastronomic preferences to the northern icefields, it is the only bear that is primarily carnivorous. Despite centuries of human predation, the polar bear population has survived—and is increasing again—filling a vast and inhospitable territory that circles the entire arctic coast, including a southerly population centered along the western shores of Hudson Bay.

Around the world, wherever humans and the bear have met throughout time, they have formed an uneasy relationship, sometimes worshipped by primitive tribes, sometimes killed for medicinal and ritual uses, often the source for myths and folktales. The bear's appeal comes not only from its shaggy, almost comic manner, but also its capacity to inspire dread. When startled, they stand on their flat-soled hind feet, sniffing the air, in a strange, humanlike posture. This behavior, rare among large mammals, is not a sign of imminent attack—though humans, not surprisingly, usually *view* it that way—but simply as a way the bear can better see and smell its surroundings. This posture has led

LEFT: *Amid the fields of lupine and fireweed of B.C.'s coastal Khutzeymateen Valley, a young bear faces—as most two- or three-year-old bears do—a life of solitude. Abandoned by its suddenly snarly mother and threatened by her new male suitors, the young bear departs. It will live or die on the skills it has acquired from its mother. Except during annual fall feeding gatherings or during brief mating periods, all bears are essentially loners.*

PREVIOUS PAGE: *Unlike many terrestrial animals, a bear's shape and lack of distinctive facial markings limit its expressiveness. With a short tail, blunt ears, and uniform coloration, the bear is a creature of streamlined simplicity. Like this pair—a mother and her cub—from northern Manitoba, all bears depend on a lowered posture, occasional growls, and snapping jaws to indicate their feelings.*

to a widespread anthropomorphic rendering of the bear as a sagacious and powerful spirit figure that is not to be taunted. Assyrian amulets from 3000 years ago show bears in this upright position wielding a raised club. The Greeks put Ursa Major, the Great Bear, into the sky where it's now known as the Big Dipper. The Romans bred bears for public gladiatorial contests.

The Navajo of the Southwest, the Haida of the Queen Charlotte Islands, the Athapaskan of Oregon, and the Inuit of the arctic all celebrated the bear as an inspiration in hunting and a powerful source of human medicine. No other animal in North America assumed such a widespread and honored position in the pantheon of tribal mythologies. The Tsimshian of northern B.C. believed the kermode—a rare, white-furred black bruin—had tremendous power as a "spirit bear." The Carrier tribe of the same region collected oil from bears' carcasses for use as a medicinal against arthritis.

In Asia, too, myth and medicine combined to attribute to various parts of the bear restorative, healing power. This belief has brought most of that continent's bears to the verge of extinction. The bear's gall bladder, when dried and powdered, is supposed to alleviate everything from headaches to heart disease to hemorrhoids. It doesn't. But the bile does dissolve human gallstones. And bear paws, served in a soup, are believed to be beneficial to people's health. Unfortunately, with a shortage of bears in Asia, poachers have turned to North America's black bears. One paw or a gall bladder can earn the hunter several hundred dollars. In Asia, a bowl of bear paw soup sells for U.S. $800 and a single gram of bear gall bladder for U.S. $50 ($1800 an ounce).

LEFT: *The black bear population in North America is recovering after 350 years of human predation. Bear bounties and poisonings have ceased and better wildlife management has allowed the black bear to reclaim areas where it had previously been eliminated. Here, a large adult scavenges among dead and dying chum salmon on a B.C. riverbank.*

Beyond the superstitions and myths, beyond the evolutionary history of the bear, lives a remarkable animal that has survived in North America, despite centuries of persecution, by its adaptability to an enormous range of climates, terrain, and food sources. Like the wolf, with whom the bear shares a number of similarities, the three species of North American bears walk out of the tundra or forest and into the human psyche because they symbolize the contradictory nature of wilderness—an unexplored place both peaceful and dangerous.

Each of the three North American bears occupies a distinct, though in places overlapping, area. The seal-eating polar bear is an inveterate wanderer, spending most of its time scanning and sniffing the ever-drifting ice, covering a circumpolar range that coincides with the Arctic Ocean and its fjord-filled shoreline. One radio-collared polar bear was tracked over a range of 300 000 square kilometres (116 000 square miles), an area larger than Oregon. Unlike the female polar bear, the male seldom dens, preferring instead to roam endlessly, even amidst the months of endless winter blackness when temperatures may drop to –57°C (–71°F) and the only light is from the aurora overhead. These very conditions have, strangely, protected the polar bear from its only real enemy: humans. Today, well protected legally, with hunting of polar bears limited to licensed aboriginals and Inuit-guided sport hunters, the species numbers 25 000 in North America.

The brown bear has had a much more tenuous relationship to humans. Since it traditionally occupied the same territory people preferred—open woodlands, valley bottoms, estuaries, and meadows—it has been the victim of constant human harrassment. Of the

two North American subspecies of the brown bear—the rare Alaskan kodiak *(Ursus arctos middendorffi)* and the grizzly *(Ursus arctos horribilis)*—the Latin name of the latter reveals mankind's view of North America's most dangerous animal. The brown bear was eliminated from most of its range in western Europe during the past millenium and from half its range in North America in the past century, as farmers, ranchers, and hunters tried to eradicate—to use a nineteenth-century, anti-bear crusader's words—"the tyrant of all animals, devouring alike man and beast." Today, the brown bear numbers 50 000 in North America, its population continuing to decrease in the face of western deforestation, habitat loss, and hunting. Its range now centers on Alaska, the Yukon, B.C. and Alberta. Still, with its massive 15-centimetre-long (6-inch) curved claws, with a weight usually between 158 and 317 kilograms (350 and 700 pounds), with a known propensity—especially among mothers with cubs—to charge intruders, with its surprising speed, the brown bear deserves the respect it usually, but not always, gets.

The forest-dwelling black bear is the most widespread, most numerous, and most adaptable of the continent's three bear species. Its range extends across the northern boreal forest south of the treeline from Alaska to Newfoundland. This range also extends southward in three fingers of black bear populations that trace the coastal mountains of the West, the Rocky Mountains, and the Appalachians. Smaller populations of this ubiquitous bear—it may number 750 000 in North America—occur in the Ozarks and the humid forests of the Gulf Coast and Florida swamps. Smaller than its other two North American counterparts, the black bear thrives by being an ursine garberator. It eats

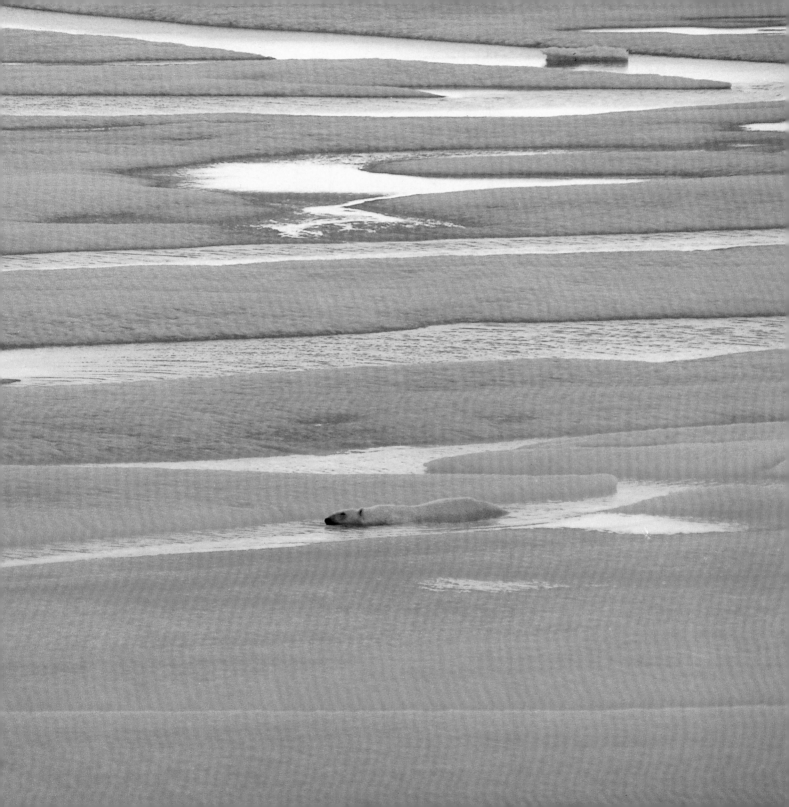

RIGHT: *Among all North American bears, the adult male is almost twice the size of the adult female. A male adult black, for example, weighs between 60 and 140 kilograms (130 and 310 pounds). An adult female weighs between 40 and 70 kilograms (90 and 155 pounds). Since the black bear population is so wide-spread and since it inhabits, in places, the periphery of human settlement, it is the continent's most seen—and most feared—large carnivore.*

practically *anything*: berries, roadkills, acorns, garbage, ants, crocodile eggs, grass, dead fish, clams, campground handouts, the occasional hapless human, and, of course, its favorite—honey.

Out in the forests of North America where the bear is usually encountered, its appearance almost inevitably provokes a sudden sequence of considerations. Although even experts may find it difficult to decide whether an encounter is threatening—an assessment the bear is also making—from a safe distance, a human observer can enjoy the creature's patient, almost lugubrious behavior. Perhaps it is September and the blueberry bushes are thick with blue-black pearls. The bear gorges, its nose snuffling among the bounty, its curled tongue stripping off the berries, packing on weight for the approaching time of denning. It is easy then, studying the bear, knowing what is ahead, to find a deeper meaning in the moment.

The bear will eat all day, every day, sometimes gaining 14 kilograms (30 pounds) a week, bulking up like a furry sumo wrestler for the six-month hibernation period. When the first deep frost hits the forest leaves, turning the blueberry bushes to mauve and the aspen along the creeks to jasmine, the bear will disappear like an apparition lost in the darkness of an early-winter snowstorm. But the bear will be nearby still, underground, sleeping, the female pregnant or nursing her new cubs, the male dreaming perhaps of early spring and the taste of skunk cabbage. In this way, the bear is like life itself, a reminder that, as Ecclesiastes said, "For everything there is a season and a time for every purpose under heaven."

RIGHT: *On the highest alpine ridges of the Rocky Mountains, the shortening, cooler days of early September turn the leaves to russet and warn the grizzly that it's time to bulk up for the approaching period underground. Mice, marmots, ground squirrels, and voles supplement a massive intake of berries. At this time of year, a grizzly may eat 20 hours a day.*

LEFT: *It's difficult to imagine that a big black bear like this one could be seriously interested in insects. But this rotting birch tree is about to be toppled and its wood ripped apart for the termites within. Bears regularly overturn rocks and dried buffalo chips looking for beetles, and rake apart anthills for their inhabitants. Wasps' nests, grasshoppers, even ladybugs... no insect is too small.*

ABOVE: *These vulnerable, young black bear cubs, just out of the den, still haven't learned to run or climb. Four months old when they first exited the den, they live at first entirely on milk and sleep until they acquire teeth and basic skills of movement.*

RIGHT: *The adult polar bear can stand 3.5 metres (11 feet) tall when rising to survey the desolate arctic tundra. Over its 20 to 25 years of life—the typical lifespan of all North American bears—the polar bear's coloration changes from the cub's white to the old-timer's creamy yellow.*

ABOVE: *The land southwest of Hudson Bay is the only place in the world where polar bears dig dens in the permafrost rather than in snowdrifts. Since the bay's ice melts—and the seals become scarce—each summer, the bears near Churchill, Manitoba are forced to fast on the land from late July to November. They use these earth dens for shelter against the summer heat and mosquitoes. Pregnant females remain ashore through the early winter to give birth in dens like this one. The mothers may not feed for eight months.*

LEFT: *About 15 kermode bears on B.C.'s remote Princess Royal Island exhibit a genetic anomaly: a rare white color phase among the island's 150 black bears. Not albinos and not polar bears, these white kermodes have lived in isolation so long that the recessive gene oddity persists. The same isolation has also produced bears that can be approached closely—if cautiously—by humans since, like the animals of Ecuador's Galapagos Islands, the animals have not learned to fear humans.*

FAR LEFT: *A mother black bear and her two grown cubs survey their Minnesota territory. While the sow is extremely protective of her young at first, she gradually relinquishes control as the cubs gain experience. By the time they are a year and a half old, she will drive them away in preparation for finding a new mate. Often, however, the cubs will temporarily rejoin their mother after the mating period is over and den near her during their first winter on their own.*

RIGHT: *In southeastern Utah, this black bear stands out against the land's eroded red rocks. Throughout its entire range,* Ursus americanus *prefers life in the forest or along its margins. With the arrival in North America of the brown bear from Asia during the last Ice Age, the black bear acquired a new foe. Today, where the two species occupy the same area, the grizzly often tries to kill the black. Since an adult grizzly can't climb trees, the black survives by heading upward at the approach of its bigger and stronger nemesis.*

ABOVE: *The front claws of a brown, or grizzly, bear are formidable weapons. They range in length from 10 to 15 centimetres (4 to 6 inches). Although its claws are usually used for digging, every year—on average—six people are mauled in North America in grizzly attacks. In fact, the grizzly shares with the tiger the distinction of being the most dangerous carnivore on Earth.*

LEFT: *The polar bear spends most of its non-hibernating time on the unimaginably featureless arctic ice. In an average lifetime it may traverse 260 000 square kilometres (100 000 square miles). How it navigates, no one knows. The ice itself is constantly drifting beneath the bear's feet. Magnetic and solar clues are often impossible to detect. There are no landmarks. Yet a female polar bear can return to her traditional denning site each autumn after six months of wandering with her cubs.*

LEFT: *Over the millenia, most bears—the exception is the polar bear—have changed from a carnivorous to a more omnivorous diet. Today, 80 to 90 percent of most grizzly or black bear sustenance comes from eating vegetation. This shift in cuisine was accompanied by the bear's development of wider, flatter molars, better suited for crushing roots, grasses, nuts, leaves, and bark to extract the nutrients within.*

FAR LEFT: *Most backcountry hikers have, at one time or another, seen this: an apprehensive black bear. In almost every case it is the bear that yields. The blacks have grown fearful of humans and are usually not aggressive unless cornered or with cubs. If a black bear attacks, however, experts advise people to fight back.*

RIGHT: *The polar bear's eyesight and hearing are as keen as a human's. But its sense of smell is perhaps unmatched in the animal kingdom. Researchers have tracked one polar bear 64 kilometres (40 miles) as it took an unwavering route—across watery leads and jumbled pressure ridges—to a seal it had apparently smelled.*

ABOVE: *Few animals can endure the frigid climate the polar bear thrives in. During an arctic blizzard, the difference between the polar bear's body temperature and the air's temperature may be 80°C (175°F).*

THE FIRST YEAR

REBIRTH: THE DEN'S DARKNESS YIELDS TO SPRING LIGHT

As the days of mid-October shorten and the first skiffs of snow dust the pines along the highest ridges, most bears of North America gradually cease their ravenous eating, as if some biological clock were slowing down. Depending on the latitude and the species, bears in different locales find a variety of solutions to the problem of the approaching cold. In the milder climates of North Carolina and Louisiana, the black bear doesn't hibernate, but merely retreats into a tree stump or subterranean den and submits to a sort of glazed "couch potato" lethargy. Farther north, almost all bears—the exception is the male polar bear—seek shelter against the suddenly diminished food supply and the snow.

Some bears—like the 150 female polar bears of the Owl River region near Churchill, Manitoba—migrate considerable distances each fall to the same denning area. Most bears, however, seek a nearby, secluded, well-drained site and begin digging. It often

PREVIOUS PAGE, LEFT: *In the Rocky Mountains, this grizzly cub faces a feast of tangy dandelions. For many bears, however, early spring is a hungry time, especially at those latitudes and altitudes where vegetation may not grow until June.*

PREVIOUS PAGE, RIGHT: *This toothless 10-day-old grizzly cub is literally helpless: its eyes and ears shut as it curls up on its mother's belly. While most newborn carnivores weigh about one-fiftieth of their adult weight, baby brown bears may weigh only one-thousandth of their future weight. This means a typical .45-kilogram (1-pound) baby could mature into a 450-kilo-gram (1000-pound) adult. (In common terms this would be the difference between a brick of butter and a large, fully loaded freezer.)*

takes the bear a week. Some big Alaskan grizzlies have been known to move a dumptruck-full load of dirt in this process. Despite *Farside* depictions to the contrary, most of these underground dens are not spacious, stalactite-filled caverns at all. Choosing a site beneath a red maple or a clump of arctic willow or a fallen cedar log or a rocky New England bluff, the bear excavates a narrow opening, often less than 30 centimetres (1 foot) across, just wide enough for the animal to squeeze through. The egg-shaped denning chamber is seldom more than 1 metre (3 feet) high and 2 metres (6 feet) long. Most polar bears select the lee side of a deep, south-facing snowdrift. Some black bears choose to hole up, literally, in hollow trees, like Winnie-the-Pooh. Still others—the bears of Pennsylvania's Pocono Mountains are known for this—find a cozy location in the crawlspace under rural cabins, nicely heated by the unsuspecting occupants above. In most cases, these dens are then insulated with twigs, leaves, and grass. Fattened from its fall gorging, secure from most predators, the bear curls up, the snow descends and blankets the den-site, and the animal drifts into a prolonged four- to seven-month sleep.

LEFT: *In this Minnesota forest, a sow bear nurses her cubs. Her nipples are the warmest part of her body and serve as nourishing targets both within the den and during the year and a half she provides her offspring with milk.*

Occasionally wolves or cougars have been seen raiding these holes. And late-denning male bears have been known to kill early-denning pregnant females. But usually this long period of dormancy passes uninterrupted. It is not, in the strictest scientific terms, "hibernation." Unlike true hibernators such as the ground squirrel, whose metabolic rate slows to near zero, the bear's body functions are simply reduced. Its metabolism drops by 50 percent, its heart rate by 80 percent, and its temperature by a few degrees. Living entirely off its body fat, losing at least one-quarter of its weight in the half-year crash diet, the bear remains virtually inert. It never drinks. It never eats. It *never once* eliminates its bodily wastes. There are occasional scientific reports—challenged by some naturalists—that the grizzly bear sometimes eats indigestible material to form a fecal plug to prevent the fouling of the den during hibernation.

Scientists are baffled by a number of features of the physiology of bear hibernation. What exactly is the chemistry of hibernation? What allows a massive animal to survive for six months without drinking, eating, excreting *once?* How is it that the bear doesn't lose any bone mass—as the bedridden, the paralyzed, and long-duration cosmonauts do—during prolonged periods of inactivity? The answers to these questions have profound implications. Understanding the chemistry of hibernation could lead not only to new treatment for people in long-term care, but to a possible cure for osteoporosis, better preservation of donated human organs, and—for that matter—the possible extension of human life itself.

For many female bears, including those with cubs and those that are pregnant, the denning time carries the additional burden of motherhood. The female has an unusual reproductive cycle called "delayed implantation." Fertilized by the male in June, she carries the free-floating embryo within her uterus for five months—without it developing beyond a microscopic cluster of cells. If the female has stored sufficient fat, the embryo finally attaches itself to the uterine wall in November and the fetus begins to grow. The scientific explanation for this phenomenon is that both male and female bears are too busy eating during the fall to spend time in courtship and breeding.

Sometime in January, at the height of winter, the female gives birth, barely awakening from her torpor. This is the only instance of hibernating mammals giving birth in the entire animal kingdom. Blind, deaf, toothless, almost bald, and utterly helpless, the babies—numbering from one to four—are the size and weight of a chipmunk. The cubs do not hibernate. The mother's reaction to the hubbub is to lick the newborns clean of their afterbirth, draw them into her fur, cup them away from the cold den floor on her curled paws, nudge them against her nipples, and fall back to sleep. For the next four months she will only awaken to reposition herself slightly, check on the cubs' well-being, and eat their excreta—a form of in-den recycling.

The cubs, for their part at first, eat and sleep. Their nursing is accompanied by a loud, sustained muttering sound that may act as a sort of auditory alarm to the comatose mother, warning her that she should not roll over and accidentally crush her tiny babies.

By six weeks, the cubs' eyes are open. By twelve weeks, they have begun to assume the fuzzy shape and rambunctious sibling goofiness so pleasing to human observers. But the mother sleeps on. As spring gradually moves northward across the continent, the force of rebirth latent in every seed and in every bear's den stirs and begins pushing toward the surface. The time underground is nearing an end.

As the days of early spring grow warmer, meltwater and sunlight seep into the den's narrow opening. First the adult male, then—a month later—the female with her cubs leave the safety of the subterranean earth for the surface and its attendant dangers. This is the worst time for the bear. Hungry wolves lurk. Aggressive, ornery male bears attack. Disease stalks the defenseless cubs. All take their toll. In fact, almost one-third of young black bears die before they reach the age of six months. The odds are worse for brown bears and worse still for young polar bears, whose first-year mortality rate is nearly 50 percent.

Depending on the latitude, sometime between late February in the south and early June in the arctic, the bear, still a little stupefied from the effects of hibernation and stiff with inactivity, pokes its nose into the fresh air. Once the groggy bear has wandered outside the den for a few hours or even days, it will need, at last, to relieve itself. One Alaskan researcher, in a moment of scatalogical curiosity, measured a post-denning grizzly's first deposit. It was 75 centimetres (30 inches) long and almost 10 centimetres (4 inches) in diameter.

LEFT: *Since the intestine of this black bear—like that of its ursine relatives—is not efficient in digesting plant material, the bear selects those parts of the plant that contain the least amount of indigestible cellulose: the roots, fruit, seeds, and flowers—like this glacier lily.*

The cubs follow their mother cautiously out of the den, their eyes adjusting to the light and their bodies to the spacious world revealed. For the first two weeks or so, all bears remain close to the den. The adults build daybeds of leaves and evergreen needles for frequent napping sessions interrupted by the occasional search for food. It is a lazy time. Black bear mothers inevitably rake together their daybed at the base of the largest nearby tree—to provide for themselves and their cubs a close, vertical route of escape from danger. All bears initially return to the den at night to sleep.

During those first months outdoors, as a few hikers have—to their dismay—learned, the sow bear is ferociously protective of her babies. The black bear may chase her own cubs up a tree and then flee there herself. Or she may—as grizzly mothers often do—charge unwitting human intruders. Backwoods wisdom says hikers should always avoid such confrontations. A bear can accelerate—in a sudden burst—to 50 kilometres per hour (30 miles per hour), a speed far faster than even an adrenalin-fueled human can run. If possible, the best route of escape is *up*— hopefully into a tree the bear itself doesn't want to climb. Studies of bear attacks show that the grizzly, although bigger and potentially more dangerous than the black bear, often mauls, but doesn't usually eat its human victim. The best defense against a grizzly attack is either to climb a tree or to "play dead" since the sow is simply defending her cubs. However, the smaller, tree-climbing black bear is, in fact, more inclined to *eat* its victim. The best defense against a black bear is fighting back.

LEFT: *A five-month-old grizzly plays amid yellow arrowleaf balsam root. For its first months outdoors, the mother and her cubs remain close to the den—in case a predatory male bear, an eagle, or a wolf appears. As summer arrives and choices of food increase, the mother will lead the cubs on an endless walkabout of her territory, introducing her children to the area's gastronomic possibilities. The location of these sites will be remembered by the bears when they are adults and the information will be passed on by the females to future generations.*

Much of the time for the cubs, however, is an idyll of feeding and playing. The sow will sit on her haunches and the cubs will nuzzle into her nipples, whipping up a creamy froth on their faces. Bloated, almost intoxicated by the rich (20 to 40 percent fat) milk, the cubs then inevitably curl up beside their equally drowsy mother, and fall asleep. Reawakened, the cubs and mother wrestle, play-fight, somersault, nip, squeal, and growl in a comic display of affectionate energy. The cubs bite their siblings. They gnaw on their own feet. They gnaw on their mother. They try tree-climbing, broken field running, and stalking tactics, half play and half practice for their lives ahead.

Gradually, the cubs acquire from their mother—the father has long disappeared—the requisite skills of survival. They learn to identify the smell and taste of the juicy, sugar-laden sapwood of spruce and pine. They climb up poplars to strip the catkins and young leaves from the branches. They learn to look for scavenging ravens and eagles circling in the blue sky—a sure sign of carrion below. And they grow fat. For example, a six-month-old black bear cub may weigh 30 kilograms (65 pounds). Even fatter, young polar bears learn the strategies of creeping along the ice on their bellies toward the snow-dens of ringed seals. Grizzly cubs, too, copy their mother as she excavates the holes of mice or marmots. The bear's acute olfactory sense leads it in ever-wider circuits, lured to new food sources as it wanders away from the denning site.

By midsummer—with the days seeming to go on forever—the mother and her charges have settled into a daily routine. It often seems that they live to play, but the

PREVIOUS PAGE: *Like other species of bears, these young polar bears learn by imitating their mother. She shows her cubs travel routes, food sites, hunting strategies, and future denning areas as the animals shuffle along at 4 kilometres per hour (2 1/2 miles per hour) over their stark territory.*

RIGHT: *As these polar bear cubs feed, they murmur a continuous, low humming sound. For their first months, they drink nothing but milk. It ranges between 32 and 48 percent fat, almost ten times as rich as human milk. Those few observers who have tasted it say the milk has the flavor of cod liver oil…or nuts.*

play is really preparation for the independent life ahead. Dozens of times a day, the cubs wrestle with each other or their mother. Sometimes the polar bear cubs—looking like pale white snowballs—take turns sliding down snowbanks on their bellies. And grizzly cubs have been observed practicing the jaw-snapping and growling techniques they have learned mean anger.

To those who have witnessed these moments of ursine parenting and childhood play, it's easy to succumb to an almost instinctive rapport with the bear. The mother is doting. The cubs are madcap. The midnight sun shines down on the slush of the sea ice off Baffin Island and reveals a mother and three cubs, walking, heads down, a little parade heading into a vast whiteness that stretches uninterrupted all the way to Siberia. In Alaska, a family of grizzlies sits in a field of lupine, patiently slurping down the flowers, the mother and her offspring like humans sucking popsicles. And a parade of black bear cubs follow their mother and a vague, new scent deep in Georgia's Okefenokee Swamp. It is a nest of alligator eggs and the promise of a full stomach.

It is hard to imagine at these moments that, within a short time, the sow will repudiate her cubs and drive them away. For a while yet, they will be members of a close family and a clan of neighboring bears. The yearling cubs will den near their mother for a second winter and grizzly cubs may stay for a third winter. But soon, they will—like all bears—head off on their own: to new areas, new food sources, new mates as the seasons tick toward adulthood and a life of perpetual wandering.

LEFT: *The McNeil River region, 300 kilometres (200 miles) southwest of Anchorage, Alaska, is the site of the world's largest annual gathering of brown bears. Naturalists have counted up to 60 bears together each summer there at the spot where the river runs shallow below a series of cascades. In the surrounding grass, this mother checks out the valley for signs of danger—in this case aggressive adult males that may be inclined to add bear cubs to their salmon diet.*

LEFT: *On the Brooks River in Alaska's Katmai National Park, these three grizzly cubs take salmon-fishing lessons from their experienced mother. The park is home to over 600 brown bears, one of the largest concentrations of the animal in the world.*

ABOVE: *The female polar bear leaves the drifting arctic pack ice to den in September or October. Snow caves—like the one here—are dug into deep drifts at the end of long tunnels. The ceiling of these multi-chambered shelters may be 3 metres (10 feet) thick. Research has shown this thickness provides enough insulation to maintain the cave's temperature at around the freezing point even when it is -34°C (-30°F) outside.*

ABOVE: *The distinctive scat of a black bear shows its diet contains a lot of berries. For most backwoods travelers, these droppings—especially if they are moist—arouse an automatic sense of heightened alertness.*

LEFT: *Just like human babies, a bear cub will suck on practically anything: a stick, its mother's ear, a tree stump, its sibling's feet, or its own toes.*

RIGHT: *This female polar bear has charged an adult male that had come too close to her cub. In fact, one of the main threats to all young bears is bloodthirsty adult males whose reproductive chances increase if the female's offspring were to die. Most males recognize the ferocity of a sow defending her cubs and flee the danger.*

RIGHT: *A cub learns from its mother the rudiments of survival. To a black bear baby, a "woof" from its mother means: climb a tree fast. An open-pawed smack on the head means: pay attention. Every gesture, every action is imitated by the cub. This Montana cub displays a threatening defensive pose.*

ABOVE: *The longest period of denning ever recorded was 8 months—for an Alaskan black bear. Most bears den 4 to 6 months. During this time the nursing mother may lose 30 kilograms (65 pounds), 40 percent of her weight. Denning consumes more time—50 percent of the bear's entire life—than any other activity. Here, three black bear cubs snuggle against their mother in a cold Minnesota winter den.*

The World of the Bear

Wandering: A Lesson in Solitude and the Lightness of Being

The bear spends much of its life as a solitary nomad, moseying around its range, generally avoiding—except at breeding time—other bears, traveling known trails, seeking known repositories of food, and scratching together in secluded sites daybeds for snoozing. But the most unique quality of the bear—and one that demonstrates its intelligence—is its legendary adaptability. The bear is known to all wildlife scientists as an extraordinarily flexible animal. It goes with the flow. It finds new solutions to problems. It scavenges. It seldom fights or defends its territory. And this is why it survives, even amid encroaching human settlement. This characteristic makes all generalizations about the bear's habits suspect. However, several patterns in the bear's social behavior do exist. It's simply a case that there are always exceptions.

Despite being a nomad, the bear does have a rough range, an area that shifts depending on, say, the failure of a salmon run on the Alaskan coast, the arrival of herds

PREVIOUS PAGE, LEFT: *In a curious anomaly of ursine behavior, some adult male polar bears develop playmates and go through a form of ritualized wrestling when they meet. This companionship begins with cautious, silent circling. Once the intent of playing is clear, the two bears gently nuzzle and chew each other in a nonthreatening way. Next, they'll rise on their hind legs, sparring, hugging, and pushing like a couple of hairy sumo wrestlers.*

PREVIOUS PAGE, RIGHT: *For some reason—not yet completely understood—both black and brown bears, especially adult males, attack certain trailside trees. This pine shows the effect of years of clawing, chewing, and scratching as local bears have created a visual and olfactory signpost in the forest. Naturalists report the bears rub their backs against the tree, then, standing on their hind legs, shimmy up and down, biting the bark over their shoulders.*

of bearded seals off Canada's Ellesmere Island, or an especially abundant crop of wild acorns, hickory, and beechnuts in eastern Tennessee. Bears of different species have ranges big enough to support their nutritional needs. For example, a male New England black bear may be content within a range of just 6.5 square kilometres (2.5 square miles). However, a male grizzly or polar bear may require—due to far sparser terrain—about 1350 square kilometres (520 square miles). And a few polar bears have ranges almost 100 times as large. On average, the much smaller female of each species, often with babies or yearlings in tow, utilizes an area only one-fourth the size of the male.

At times, however, the animals congregate in a most un-bearlike manner. At the famous McNeil River Falls on the Alaskan peninsula, as many as 60 grizzlies regularly gather to haul salmon from the rapids there. On the western shore of Hudson Bay, over 100 polar bears wait together for the annual freeze-up of the sea ice. And in the northern Rockies, naturalists have counted a dozen black bears together, all munching huckle-

LEFT: *This Alaskan grizzly is standing on its half-buried adult caribou kill. Unlike black bears that never cache their prey, the brown bear may hide, even sleep on, and vigorously defend its prey against other predators. In some places, research shows that grizzlies kill 40 percent of the calves of local deer, elk, and caribou.*

berries without signs of conflict. In fact, some of these bears do fight—over a favorite salmon-fishing hole, over threats made toward the cubs, or out of natural surliness. It seems that bears, like humans, have personalities—some are placid, some generous, some fearful, and some just plain nasty. But usually, a hierarchy, understood among neighboring bears, prevails: the big, dominant males on top, then the females with cubs, then the single females, and lastly the cubs. Except during times of food shortages or abundance or the female bear's two-month-long breeding season, the bear prefers to avoid contact with other members of its species.

It's during the June breeding season that the bear is most likely to overcome its predisposition to solitude. Adult males begin cruising—in hopes of finding a female in heat. Even the estrous female sometimes cruises, looking for a suitable mate. When a male catches a whiff of eau-de-ursine, left on the female's daybed or wherever she has urinated, he begins to follow his nose. The smell's effect is intoxicating. Soon, however, every nearby male has descended on the female, producing a parade of swaggering, feisty contenders. The dominant male will do his best—often not good enough—to chase away other suitors. Vicious fights, often producing severe wounds, are not uncommon. Meanwhile, the female, typically half the size of testosterone-crazed males, reacts to the sudden attention by fleeing. Over a period of several days, though, she allows a brief courtship to develop with the dominant male. Nuzzling and play-wrestling are normal bear foreplay. Repeated half-hour-long sessions of intercourse follow. For these three to five days, it seems as if a family bond has been established. The two bears travel, eat, and sleep together. But in the end, the male lumbers off, looking for other females to pursue. In some recorded cases, a male may mate with a half-dozen different females in a day. And the female may mate with several other partners before she, too, returns to the nomadic life.

As the summer slowly passes, life for the three species of North American bear assumes old and solitary patterns. The adult polar bear carries inside its head the knowledge of survival in a land where few other terrestrial creatures live. For twelve hours a day, it travels alone—its eyes slitted against the sun, its nose into the wind, shuffling along—guided in the barren landscape of drifting ice and glaciated islands by hunger, experience, and an incredibly sensitive nose that can detect the smell of a seal 32 kilometres (20 miles) away. Two million ringed seals—the polar bear's favorite prey—live in the arctic, basking alongside leads and meltwater channels, their eyes alert to the hulking approach of their enemy. The polar bear is a skilled swimmer. Its long, pointed head, its paddle-shaped paws, its 10 centimetres (4 inches) of blubber and its thick matting of hollow hairs allow it to cross narrow, icy channels in a sudden burst of fury or frigid 80-kilometre-wide (50-mile) straits in a day's steady swimming. No one knows how the polar bear navigates in such a featureless world, but when it closes in on a seal, all its strategems and patience are put to the test. It's not uncommon for a polar bear to go a week or two without a single kill.

Often a polar bear will stalk a seal and capture it as it surfaces at a breathing hole. Or it may float motionlessly in the water, mimicking an ice patch until a seal nears it.

Sometimes a polar bear will stalk a seal across the ice. When it nears its quarry, the bear drops its chin and slithers snakelike across the ice, propelled forward by its hind feet. It hides behind ridges and hummocks, skulking silently, trying to remain unnoticed until it is within 30 metres (100 feet). Then: it charges. In three out of four cases, the seal escapes. If the bear is fortunate, it sends the seal airborne with a single swipe of its massive left paw—for polar bears are all lefties. The hunt is over. Scientists have watched in awe as particularly hungry bears have eaten an entire 70-kilogram (150-pound) seal—flippers, claws, bones, and all—in a single orgy of eating.

When food is abundant, scientists also report that polar bears, like wolves, may kill for sport. Baby whitecoat seals become instructive toys batted between a sow and her cubs. And narwhals and huge beluga whales, trapped in icy pools called *savssats*, may be slaughtered by polar bears indiscriminately, their bodies then abandoned in a display of arctic bloodlust.

Mostly though, the polar bear walks and walks—one radio-tagged specimen covered 3200 kilometres (2000 miles) in a single year—a lonely, cream-colored creature noticed only, if at all, by bands of Inuit also hunting on the ice. These people have recorded the ghostly presence of the animal in their mythologies and religious ceremonies. They call the bear *Nanook*. Their artwork has—through the centuries—transformed it into scrimshaw images, soapstone carvings, and the strange, raised *inukshuks*, rough stone towers that imitate a standing polar bear's posture and have served as landmarks for native travelers for millenia.

LEFT: *Polar bears ride the slowly drifting arctic ice on its perpetual clockwise rotation around the North Pole. Their primary source of nutrition is seals, although on occasion they also hunt walrus and musk oxen. Usually solitary predators, groups of polar bears are drawn to beached dead whales—as here— where this mother and her grown cub tussle over the bloody spoils.*

Far to the south, the black bear, too, walks endlessly and more noticed because of its numbers and the habitat it occupies. Unlike the other two species of North American bears, the black bear's visibility is heightened by the fact that it shows more variations of color than any other carnivore on earth. So, although known scientifically as the American black bear, this species' coloration ranges from the blue-grey "glacier bear" of southeastern Alaska to the rare and placid, yellow-white kermode bear of B.C.'s central coast to the brown-colored black bear of Arizona to the truly black-furred black bear of Florida and many other areas of North America.

Because of its enormous range, the black bear's habits and diet reflect both millions of years of occupancy of the continent and its adaptations to the forested terrain it prefers. It is, in that way, North America's preeminent tree-hugger, choosing to live along the wood's margins where a wide range of food is available and safety is never farther than a tree trunk away. Relatively small, agile, with short, curved claws and powerful hind legs, the black bear's tree-climbing ability is one of the distinctive differences between it and the other two North American bear species. (Very young brown bears climb trees, too, but mature grizzlies lose that skill.) Although the main threat to the blacks is from humans—hunters kill thousands every year—the black bear will also flee upward from an approaching grizzly, its lethal archenemy, or a rogue black male trying to kill a mother or her cubs. In fact, a sow and her cubs will often nurse and sleep in trees, draping themselves over the higher branches like shag rugs hung out to dry.

LEFT: *On a hot day, a black bear's thick coat is as much a nuisance as it is essential during winter weather. During the warmest days, a bear will seek the comforts of a riverbank, browsing for food and taking frequent five-minute-long wallows in shallow pools. Unlike dogs, however, a bear will not shake the water off, preferring to remain wet and cool as long as possible.*

The trees' leaves, catkins, nuts, fruit, and sugar-rich sapwood are a major source of a black bear's nutrition. And the wood's inhabitants—ants, honey bees, and myriad beetles—are like multi-legged vitamin pills, important dietary supplements. Moreover, an adult male uses certain, specific trees as so-called "rubbing trees" or "blaze trees," clawing at the bark, rubbing against the wood, urinating on the roots, biting the trunks repeatedly as if creating a series of ursine signposts throughout its territory. These are not, apparently, markers of any boundaries since the bear does this throughout its range. The tree-marking's purpose is, in fact, unknown. But in places the same tree has been used by generations of bears for over 200 years.

By early September, the black—like its two North American counterparts—goes on a serious eating binge, often bulking up 1 to 2 kilograms (2 to 4 pounds) a day. Through the course of the next two months a pregnant female may double her weight and a Pennsylvanian male is reported to have gained during one monstrous fall eating orgy, 58 kilograms (128 pounds). Ninety percent of this food is vegetation. In the east, the black bear climbs trees, snapping off limbs, devouring the nuts and fruit, before discarding them on the ground. In Oregon and Washington, the black may clearcut a meadow of alpine flowers.

But everywhere, the black bear consumes copious—no, gargantuan—amounts of berries. Salmonberries, crowberries, salal berries, huckleberries, blueberries, mountain ash berries, and the appropriately named bearberries—all are grist for the voracious,

PREVIOUS PAGE: *Two families of polar bears—plus one loner—congregate on the sea ice near Churchill, Manitoba waiting for the fall freeze-up. Most polar bears in the high arctic live permanently on the frozen Arctic Ocean, following the edges of the sea ice as it slowly extends southward. However, the polar bears of the Churchill region—seen by over 10 000 tourists each year—remain on or close to the land. During the summer months they move inland and dig caves into the permafrost to keep cool, then head out onto Hudson Bay as the ocean freezes each October.*

RIGHT: *Although called the black bear,* Ursus americanus *ranges in color from the rare, yellow-white kermode bear of the central B.C. coast to the auburn-colored bear of the U.S. southwest to the obsidian-colored bear found throughout North America. Here a cinnamon-colored black bear rummages for insects in a rotten log in Montana.*

ursine mill. As most backcountry hikers know, a bear in a berry patch is an animal close to heaven. Part of the reason the bear slurps down so many berries—it may feast nonstop for hours—is that its digestive system was not designed for a vegetarian life. With a short intestine and no capacity, as sheep and other ruminants have, to redigest its food, the bear must become a four-legged, wilderness vacuum cleaner, processing millions of berries each autumn. What's curious about this is the bear doesn't *chew* the berries, it *gulps* them down whole. This is because some berries taste very sour and others contain tiny seeds that, if crushed, would release poisonous toxins into the bear's system. This means—as the close inspection of a bear's distinctive blackish scat would reveal—the berry seeds pass through the animal's digestive tract more or less unaffected. The "more or less" is also interesting. The enzymes in the bear's stomach *do* strip some of the hull off certain seeds, which—when excreted—tend to germinate faster than similar seeds that have not been similarly processed. Raspberries reproduce twice as frequently, chokeberries three times as frequently, and dogwood seven times as frequently if their seeds have taken this slightly more roundabout route to the soil.

By this time, all across North America, the young bears have been weaned and educated in wilderness strategies. They are then peremptorily driven away, amid woofing and snapping jaws, by their suddenly disinterested mother. For a while, the young siblings may work as a team, fishing for coho salmon or raiding a lucrative blueberry patch, even sleeping together. Soon though, the cycle of solitary wandering begins for

the youngsters as each bear finds a new range and lives or dies by the lessons it has learned previously.

As the day's light shortens and Ursa Major rises overhead earlier each night, the brown bear, too, commences its annual pilgrimage to those sites, first seen at its mother's heels, where it will find food. The grizzly is built for digging. With its massive, muscular shoulders—seen in profile as its distinctive hump—it frequently pursues mice, marmots, and gophers into their burrows, hurling spadefuls of dirt backward as it trenches furiously after its prey. An Alaskan grizzly was observed catching 357 ground squirrels one fall as it fattened itself for hibernation. The brown bear has been known, as well, to loot the underground food caches of singing voles and to burrow for the nutritious roots of glacier lilies and wild onions.

But the brown bear of coastal North America holds a special place in its heart for salmon. By August, the first runs have begun and by September the rivers are full of spawning sockeye and coho. Faced with a glut of food and a biological compulsion to EAT, the bear positions itself amid shallow rapids and gorges on the migrating fish. It may employ a run-and-scatter technique, driving the frightened fish before it. It may snorkle, its head submerged, its nostrils trailing bubbles as it chases its prey. It may hook the salmon with its claws. Or it may wait patiently at a waterfall until a salmon becomes airborne, then snag the fish in its mouth like a dog catching a frisbee.

At the height of this feeding frenzy, the grizzly may eat 20 hours daily. It is not unheard of, naturalists report, for a successful grizzly to catch 10 salmon an hour and up

LEFT: *In Alaska's Katmai National Park, four brown bears hunt for salmon as the ubiquitous gulls wait for leftovers. From mid-July onward into fall, a huge sockeye salmon run lures bears and tourists to Brooks Falls, where an elevated public-viewing platform has been built. Although humans and bears come into close proximity here, there has been only one mishap: to a camper who had carelessly wiped bacon grease onto his posterior.*

OVERLEAF: *At low tide, this remote beach in Alaska's volcanic Katmai National Park is a perfect place for gathering marine life. Here, one of the park's 600 grizzlies craters the sand, excavating a fresh clam from each hole.*

to 100 a day. All this activity inevitably draws other animals to the feeding site. Bald eagles circle, ravens and seagulls dive-bomb, wolves stand poised, all descending on the prime feasting spots in a natural gathering of carnivores and carrion-eaters. The bear, at the top of the food chain, has no reason to fear. It just eats and eats.

When the bear has feasted and has attained the girth of an earth-bound blimp, it is forced by its internal physiology to consider what lies ahead. There's a coldness in the evening air. And snow on the highest peaks. The bear then trudges inland, upward, following, at first, ancient and rutted trails in the coastal rainforest and the mountain tundra. These routes are worn deep with the regular footprints of generations of bears whose passage today, and 10, 50, 200 years ago have left a visible record on the land. These trails radiate outward from the popular feasting sites like country roads leading away from a pub.

Gradually, the bear disperses into the wilderness where it resumes its singular and self-sufficient life. Soon, it will head into the earth for its winter hibernation. There, it takes on the aura of myth. Asleep, hidden in its subterranean world, it becomes a shadowy reminder of the spirituality of nature's endless cycles and a lesson to modern humans, as it was to Neolithic man 30 000 years ago, that the darkness of winter is not forever. For things hidden, things underground are transformed and reborn again with the spring. The reappearing mother bear, with her cubs in tow, is a symbol of life's circularity—that out of the earth itself comes the source of new life.

RIGHT: *A perpetual problem for the bear is that its solitary life makes it difficult to find a mate. The male starts looking for a female weeks before the mid-summer breeding season begins. The cubs are born 225 or so days after copulation, but the fetus is at that time only 60 days old. This is because a process called delayed implantation halts the pregnancy after the eggs are fertilized, but before they attach themselves to the uterine wall. It is only when the female is fat and ready for denning—five months after copulation—that the bear's embryos implant and fetal development recommences.*

FAR RIGHT: *The only time most adult bears socialize is during the two-month-long summer breeding season. Here a male and female grizzly scrounge for insects together in a prelude to mating. For four or five days, they will appear inseparable. But, after intercourse, they will each wander off, looking for others to mate with.*

RIGHT: *Seldom seen on their remote, rainforest-covered island 500 kilometres (300 miles) northwest of Vancouver, the rare kermode bear has yellow-white fur, ivory-colored claws, brown eyes, and a black nose. Naturalists who have spent time with the kermode report the animals are so friendly they may, out of curiosity, smudge a photographer's lens with their nose and allow people to tickle their belly with a stick.*

ABOVE: *A grizzly will excavate the tunnels of its prey with lethal, curved claws. In fact, the grizzly's pronounced shoulder-hump is formed of muscles built precisely for digging. This mother, having caught a ground squirrel, eats it while her two cubs wait patiently for some scraps.*

LEFT: *This grizzly sow, with her cub watching from behind her, trenches after an arctic ground squirrel on the Alaskan tundra. In the fall, bears are relentless in their pursuit of food. Polar bears may stake out seals' aglos—breathing holes—for hours or days, waiting for their prey to appear. Blacks will rip apart an entire log, licking the termites out. Five grizzlies in Canada's Northwest Territories ate over 24 000 eggs in a single, determined orgy of eating.*

ABOVE: *As with North America's other ursine species, the black bear knows the location and the time various foods reach maturity. Whether it is—as here—the September ripening of mountain ash berries along a Minnesota creek or the location of an acorn-filled oak grove in northern Maine, the bear can locate the site with an accuracy based on years, even generations, of experience.*

RIGHT: *Throughout North America, the bear is at the top of the food chain, threatened in most cases only by human hunters or the occasional marauding male bear. Walruses have been known to kill polar bears. Wolves and bald eagles have been seen attacking bear cubs. But most wild animals—this arctic fox is an exception—steer clear of bears because of their enormous strength and carnivorous proclivities.*

LEFT: *The salmon runs on the continent's northwest coast are a bonanza for the region's bears. Come late July, August, and September, millions of migrating salmon head upriver to spawn. Each bear has its favorite site and returns to the exact spot year after year. Observers at the McNeil River site in Alaska recorded that one brown bear—a grizzly nicknamed Groucho—caught 88 salmon there in one day and 1018 in the course of one season.*

ABOVE: *By the time they reach age two, most bears have begun a life of solitude. This young black bear has been chased away by its mother and must find in some distant part of her territory a place to call its own. Once settled, it will avoid other bears, but— unlike the wolf—it won't defend its new territory, preferring to mosey away from other ursine intruders rather than to fight.*

EPILOGUE

THE BEAR'S LURKING PRESENCE: THE POWER OF POSSIBILITIES

To those who have spent time in the wilderness, the sudden appearance of a bear often becomes a source of stories told around campfires years later. No other wild, North American creature—not the shy wolf, not the elusive mountain lion—commands such a power. Because it is big and strong, because it sometimes does—unlike the much-maligned wolf—kill people, because it lives throughout much of the continent, the bear is a force to be reckoned with. During most of the time that humans and bears have occupied North America, the bear found favor among the tribal peoples as a mystical animal. It was often celebrated. The Kwakiutl carved its broad face into their totem poles. The Cree of the Great Plains, observing the bear's propensity for standing on its rear legs, were convinced the animal had supernatural powers. They wore bear claws as talismans and feasted on bear hearts to acquire courage. Throughout its range, its springtime resurrection from within the earth was seen as a message of renewal.

PREVIOUS PAGE, LEFT: *Canada still allows controlled, subsistence polar bear hunting by Inuit or by southern sport hunters who buy into the Inuit quota. Despite these legal kills, the polar bear seems to be making a comeback after 350 years of human predation.*

PREVIOUS PAGE, RIGHT: *A male black bear follows a bear trail through Minnesota woodlands in the early fall. In places, these trails are rutted 30 centimetres (1 foot) deep or pitted with the regular footsteps of generations of passing bears. The trails crisscross the bear's range and lead to known sites for eating, bathing, and certain "bear trees" the animals ritually scar with their claws. In the Pacific Northwest, these rutted trails, marked by impressive 35-centimetre (14-inch) grizzly footprints, are—almost certainly—the source of the Bigfoot or Sasquatch legends.*

The arrival 350 years ago of white settlers marked the opening chapter in an almost ceaseless war—fought with poison, traps, and guns—against the continent's bears. Cast as a ferocious villain in the black bear country of Appalachia, as a consummate killer in the grizzly-filled mountains of the nineteenth-century west, and as a white monster that would appear out of the polar gloom to eat its victims and to unearth the graves of human dead, the bear died by the hundreds of thousands, probably millions. The goal then was to eliminate all vestiges of such a beast from the land. Brown and black bears lost almost half their territory. The polar bear population plummeted as early whalers killed bears for meat, skins, and sport.

It was, of course, one of those tragic aspects of a society bent on conquering a new land and subduing its creatures to the will of agriculture, ranching, and—in the end—suburbia and strip-malls. The bear retreated where possible. It grew justifiably fearful of its new nemesis. It sought the safety of the remotest forests and alpine ridges where few people went.

LEFT: *Most bears punctuate their day with naps, usually in a thicket or dense bushes where they are unseen. When a bear beds down in the summer months, it often rakes together a pile of grass, moss, and leaves for its day bed. It does not sleep in a den. Here, a black bear curls up in a cedar swamp during an early autumn rain.*

But in recent decades, as the wilderness has laid an ever-greater claim on the psyche of modern North Americans, the bear has been restored as a creature worthy of respect and reverence. It's almost as if the bear is seen, at some subconscious level, as an accurate reflection of the hidden, the numinous, the darker side of human nature. It *can* be dangerous. But its preference is to be left alone. As people today push into the farthest reaches of the western wilderness, they find the grizzly still prevails. As tourists and adventurers penetrate the arctic's barrenness, the polar bear prevails. Just as the black bear prevails not far beyond those places where the last dimly lit houses yield to empty, forest-lined, two-lane country roads. In this way, the bear is a reminder to humans of the dark and soulful side of things. The possibility of the bear—out there someplace in the blackness—adds poignancy to every trip into those untamed places where electricity ends and the fundamentals begin. The bear makes the wilderness darker, the sounds of the forest sharper, the wind more ominous, and the mountain ridges steeper. The possibility of the bear elevates the senses, just as it elevates the human mind to the presence of danger and revelation.

LEFT: *Except during the mid-winter denning period, a female and her cubs sleep outside, even during arctic gales. Snow coats their fur and drifts over their bodies, but the animals' thick coats and layers of fat protect them from the cold.*

LEFT: *Some bears are nocturnal, some diurnal, and some are most active—in bear psychology, this means* eating—*during the crepuscular light of dawn and dusk. But in the autumn feeding frenzy, all bears eat more or less continuously, some even gaining 1.5 to 3 kilograms (3 to 6 pounds) a day in weight.*

FAR LEFT: *Most bears have little need to communicate, and so are often silent. Black bears, living in forested environments where visibility is poor, are the most vocal of North America's bears. A mother "huffs" to send her cubs fleeing up a tree and grunts to call them back down. Male black bears growl and bellow when involved in mating fights. But grizzly and polar bears, living in more open environments, depend on visual cues to communicate. They seldom make any sounds.*

ABOVE: *The brown bear has commanded the respect of humans through time. Native North American bear hunters would pray to the bear before killing it, asking it not to take revenge on the hunters in its afterlife. They would place the bear skull atop a tall pole and hang its bones in bark baskets from tree limbs. They'd call the bear "grandfather," a term of great respect. Certain tribes used the image of the bear's broad-faced head in totem poles and considered themselves human members of the bear clan.*

LEFT: *On Alaska's Toklat River, this female grizzly surveys a landscape virtually un-changed since the end of the Ice Age 10 000 years ago. Both the North American grizzly and polar bear population are considered "vulnerable" by scientists. Neither species numbers more than 50 000. Strict hunting limits on both these species mean their populations are stable at present. Over 25 000 black bears are shot by North American hunters each year, but—because of the black bear's fecundity and omnivorous habits—this population actually seems to be growing.*

RIGHT: *The bear's shuffling gait is unusual among mammals. Most animals walk on their toes. But the bear—like the raccoon, porcupine, beaver, and human—walks flat-footed with its heels touching the ground. Most polar bears roam the periphery of the arctic ice, where seals are plentiful. However, polar bear footprints have been found within two degrees of the North Pole and one marked polar bear was found to have crossed the arctic, covering 3200 kilometres (2000 miles) in one year.*

FAR RIGHT: *Polar bears are exceptional swimmers, capable of speeds of 10 kilometres per hour (6 miles per hour) over nonstop distances of 100 kilometres (60 miles). They swim with their webbed forepaws and use their hind feet as rudders. On those occasions when a mother is crossing a watery lead in the ice, her young cubs frequently ride atop her since they haven't acquired the blubbery layer of older cubs.*

RIGHT: *With Alaska's Mount McKinley as a backdrop, this grizzly heads upslope on its perpetual quest for food. Omnivorous like humans, the various species of bears have survived —until their recent extermination in many areas by* Homo sapiens—*through eating almost anything edible in their path.*

RIGHT: *Like some other north-ern animals, the bear will retreat to mid-river pools to escape the incessant bombard-ment of mosquitoes.*

FAR RIGHT: *Despite its fierce reputation, the grizzly—say the experts—wants to be left alone. It seldom attacks people. But because of its impressive size—some stand 1.5 metres (5 feet) at the shoulder and are 2.5 metres long (over 8 feet)—humans have a jus-tifiable fear of the creature. It has been nearly eliminated in all the western United States except Alaska. Several small pockets of grizzlies survive in Wyoming's Yellowstone National Park and along the border joining Washington, Idaho and Montana with Canada. Some effort is now being directed into relocating Canadian grizzlies into the western U.S.*

LEFT: *The black bear, the only one of the three North American bears with a lengthy history on the continent, has been driven out of some of its traditional ranges in the north by the bigger and more aggressive newcomer—the brown bear. But if the brown is eradicated in an area—as happened 150 years ago in Labrador and Quebec's Ungave Peninsula—the black repopulates its old territory.*

FAR LEFT: *The ice fields and ice floes of the Arctic Ocean are home to the polar bear's main prey: bearded, ringed, and hooded seals. This diet is supplemented with seaweed, clams, crabs, and fish collected while the animal is diving. They also eat carrion, such as dead whales, washed ashore on arctic coastlines. Most polar bears weigh in at 450 kilograms (1000 pounds), although one caught and measured recently in Canada's high arctic weighed 950 kilograms (2100 pounds).*

SUGGESTED READING

Cox, Daniel. 1990. *Black Bear*. San Francisco: Chronicle.

Domico, Terry. 1988. *Bears of the World*. New York: Oxford.

Feazel, Charles T. 1990. *White Bear*. New York: Henry Holt.

Ford, Barbara. 1981. *Black Bear: The Spirit of the Wilderness*. Boston: Houghton Mifflin.

Lynch, Wayne. 1993. *Bears: Monarchs of the Northern Wilderness*. Vancouver: Greystone.

Murray, John A. 1992. *The Great Bear*. Anchorage: Alaska Northwest Books.

Russell, Andy. 1967. *Grizzly Country*. New York: Knopf.

Shepard, Paul and Barry Sanders. 1985. *The Sacred Paw*. New York: Viking Press.

Van Wormer, Joe. 1966. *The World of the Black Bear*. Philadelphia: J.B. Lippincott.

INDEX

Bold entries refer to photographs.

PHOTO CREDITS

Daniel J. Cox/Natural Exposures vi–vii, 2–3, 4–5, 14–15, 18, 22, 24, 26–27, 30, 31, 34–35, 36–37, 40–41, 44–45, 54–55, 56, 57, 62–63, 65, 70–71, 72–73, 78, 81, 82, 83, 84–85, 87, 89, 90–91, 98, 104

Thomas Kitchin/First Light x, 8–9, 16–17, 25, 79

Patrick Morrow/First Light 1

Tom Ellison/First Light 6

Lynn M. Stone 10–11, 74, 76–77, 96

Ian Stirling 13, 21, 51

Robert Lankinen/First Light 19, 20, 58, 88

Ron Thiele 23, 80

Tim Christie 28, 29, 39, 42, 52, 53, 59, 68, 95, 97, 102, 103

Victoria Hurst/First Light 32

Leonard Lee Rue III 33

Bryan & Cherry Alexander/First Light 46–47

Charles Campbell/First Light 48–49

Jim Zuckerman/First Light 50

Len Rue, Jr. 60–61, 100–101, 105

Fred Bruemmer 66–67

Wayne Lynch 86, 92–93, 99

Stephen Homer/First Light 94